BRIGHT IDEA BOOKS

T0009121

MICHAEL B.
Jordan

by Celina McManus

CAPSTONE PRESS
a capstone imprint

Bright Ideas is published by Capstone Press, an imprint of Capstone.
1710 Roe Crest Drive
North Mankato, Minnesota 56003
www.capstonepub.com

Copyright © 2020 by Capstone. All rights reserved. No part of this publication may be reproduced in whole or in part, or stored in a retrieval system, or transmitted in any form or by any means, electronic, mechanical, photocopying, recording, or otherwise, without written permission of the publisher.

Library of Congress Cataloging-in-Publication Data
Names: McManus, Celina, 1992- author.
Title: Michael B. Jordan / by Celina McManus.
Description: North Mankato, Minnesota : Capstone Press, [2020] | Series: Influential People | Includes index. | Audience: Grades: 4-6
Identifiers: LCCN 2019029498 (print) | LCCN 2019029499 (ebook) | ISBN 9781543590807 (hardcover) | ISBN 9781496665874 (paperback) | ISBN 9781543590814 (ebook)
Subjects: LCSH: Jordan, Michael B. (Michael Bakari), 1987—Juvenile literature. | African American actors—United States—Biography—Juvenile literature.
Classification: LCC PN2287.J68 M36 2020 (print) | LCC PN2287.J68 (ebook) | DDC 791.43/028—dc2 3
LC record available at https://lccn.loc.gov/2019029498
LC ebook record available at https://lccn.loc.gov/2019029499

Image Credits
Alamy: Gregorio Binuya/Everett Collection, 8, Remi Agency/Entertainment Pictures, 11; AP Images: Ian West/PA Wire URN:41422345/Press Association, cover; Getty Images: Johnny Nunez/WireImage, 7; iStockphoto: FangXiaNuo, 31; Newscom: Jim Ruymen/UPI, 22–23; Rex Features: B Wetcher/MGM/Warner Bros/Kobal, 15, David Lee/HBO/Blown Deadline/Kobal, 12, Marvel/Disney/Kobal, 5; Shutterstock Images: Joe Seer, 27, 28, Kathy Hutchins, 24, Kobby Dagan, 19, Paul Smith/Featureflash Photo Agency, 16, Tinseltown, 21
Design Elements: Shutterstock Images

Editorial Credits
Editor: Charly Haley; Designer: Laura Graphenteen; Production Specialist: Colleen McLaren

All internet sites appearing in back matter were available and accurate when this book was sent to press.

Printed in the United States of America.
PA99

TABLE OF CONTENTS

CHAPTER 1

BECOMING HIS
Character

Michael B. Jordan closed his eyes. He thought about what his character was like. He wrote about him in a journal. He spent time alone. He became Erik Killmonger.

Jordan played the character Erik in the movie *Black Panther*. Jordan worked to become this character. Jordan helped pick some clothes for Erik. He also exercised a lot. This helped him look like Erik. Erik is just one of the characters Jordan has become. Jordan thinks a lot about his characters.

Michael B. Jordan as Erik Killmonger in *Black Panther*

CHAPTER 2

GROWING Up

Jordan was born in California in 1987. Then his family moved to Newark, New Jersey. Growing up in Newark was hard sometimes. Some of Jordan's friends got into trouble. But Jordan wanted to stay safe and follow the rules. His parents helped him.

Jordan still lived in Newark at the beginning of his acting career. He later moved back to California.

Jordan started out as a model and actor.

Jordan started modeling at age 10. He was in newspaper ads. His mom took him to **auditions**. Soon he got an acting **role**. He acted in a TV commercial.

DANCING

Jordan did not always know he wanted to act. His parents let him try different things. He took tap dancing classes when he was young.

CHAPTER 3

ACTING

Jordan kept auditioning for acting roles. He started getting small parts in TV shows.

Jordan got his first big role in 2001. It was for the movie *Hardball*. He played a baseball player.

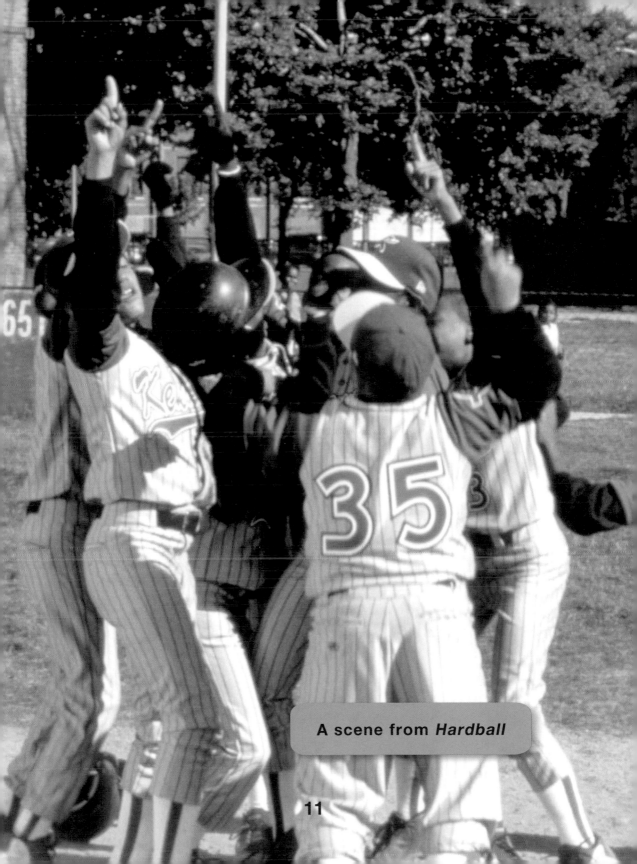

A scene from *Hardball*

Jordan (left) in
The Wire

In 2002 Jordan got another big role. He played Wallace in the TV show *The Wire*. Jordan thought about Wallace a lot. He liked the story his character told.

Jordan acted in more movies and TV shows. He was a high school quarterback in the show *Friday Night Lights*. He was in the show *Parenthood* too.

Then in 2015 Jordan starred in the movie *Creed*. He played a **boxer**. The movie won awards.

In 2018 Jordan got the role of Erik in *Black Panther*. He worked hard to make the character come to life.

Jordan played a boxer named Adonis in the movie *Creed*.

Jordan (left) at an event with his mom (center) and sister

SUCCESS

Jordan became a successful actor. He had always dreamed of buying a home for his parents. He made this dream come true. He bought a house. He lived there with his parents for three years. He was able to take care of them.

Jordan has also started working as a movie **producer**. He wants to make movies that show more people of color.

VOICE ACTING

Jordan does voice acting too. He was the voice of a character in the video game *Gears of War 3.*

Jordan (left) talks with actors Kate Mara (center) and Jamie Bell. Jordan works with many people in Hollywood.

19

CHAPTER 4

MAKING A
Difference

Jordan says his parents taught him to be kind. They taught him to care about others. This is why Jordan works hard. He wants his characters to tell important stories.

Jordan (right) and his mom at the Academy Awards in 2019

Jordan (second from right) with his *Black Panther* costars in 2019

But Jordan also uses his success to make a difference in the world. In 2018 Jordan helped create a rule at a big movie company. The rule makes sure people of color are picked to work on big movies. It means more people of color will get lead roles. The rule is the first of its kind.

Jordan (second from left) with his family at an event for Lupus LA

HELPING OTHERS

Sometimes helping others begins at home. Jordan's mom has an illness called lupus. It causes pain in a person's body. Jordan works to help people with lupus like his mom. He works with the group Lupus LA. The group raises money for people with the illness.

Jordan connects with his characters. He plays characters with meaningful stories. He uses his fame to help people. Jordan will continue acting and helping people.

Jordan likely has a successful career ahead of him.

GLOSSARY

audition
a tryout for an acting role or modeling job

boxer
a person who participates in boxing, a fighting sport that involves punching a bag or a partner

producer
a person who manages money or other parts of making a movie

role
the character that an actor plays

TIMELINE

1987: Michael B. Jordan is born.

2001: Jordan gets his first big acting role with the movie *Hardball*.

2002: Jordan is in *The Wire*.

2016: Jordan buys a house for his parents.

2018: Jordan plays Erik Killmonger in *Black Panther*.

2018: Jordan helps create a rule at a big Hollywood company to have more people of color in big movie roles.

ACTIVITY

CREATE A CHARACTER

Michael B. Jordan loves playing different characters. When he played Erik Killmonger in *Black Panther*, he thought about what the character's life was like. He wrote it down. You can do this too! Make up a character. Write down your character's story. What does he or she look like? Where does he or she live? What are his or her favorite things? After you write about the character, you can act! Show your friends or family members how you can act like this character you created.

FURTHER RESOURCES

Want to learn more about *Black Panther*? Check out these resources:

Black Panther Official Website
https://www.marvel.com/movies/black-panther

Snider, Brandon T. *Battle For Wakanda*. Los Angeles, Calif.: Marvel, 2019.

Zalewski, Aubrey. *Chadwick Boseman*. North Mankato, Minn.: Capstone Press, 2020.

Interested in acting? Learn more with these resources:

Bell, Samantha S. *You Can Work in Movies*. North Mankato, Minn.: Capstone Press, 2019.

Wonderopolis: Can Anyone Be an Actor?
https://www.wonderopolis.org/wonder/can-anyone-be-an-actor

INDEX